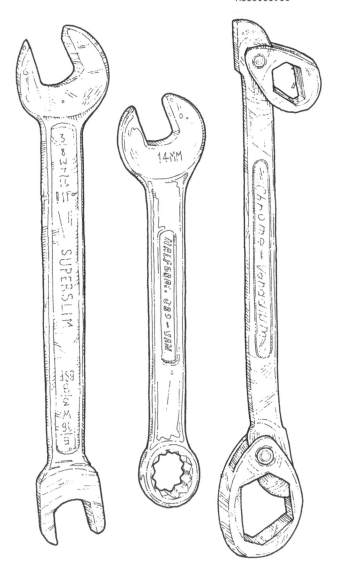

Published in 2016 by
Laurence King Publishing Ltd
361-373 City Road
London EC1V 1LR
United Kingdom
Tel: +44 20 7841 6900
Fax: +44 20 7841 6910

e-mail: enquiries@laurenceking.com
www.laurenceking.com

ISBN: 978-1-78067-901-3

Printed in China

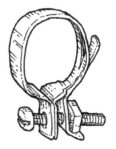

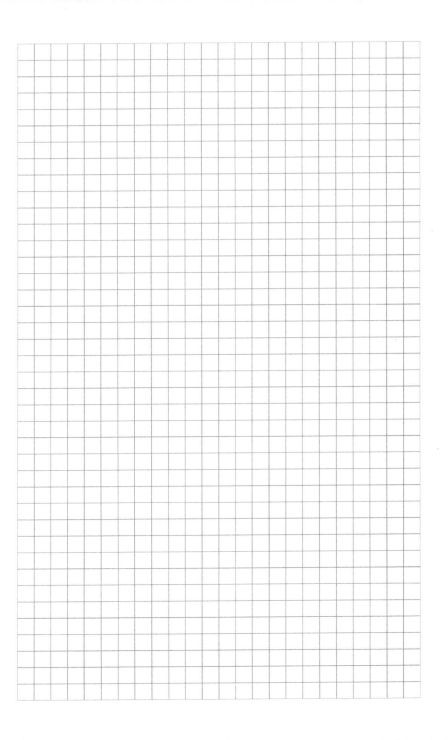

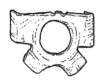

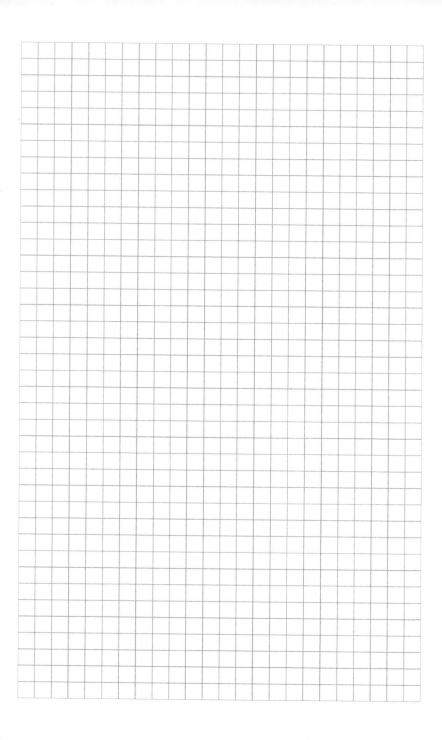

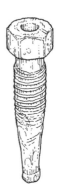

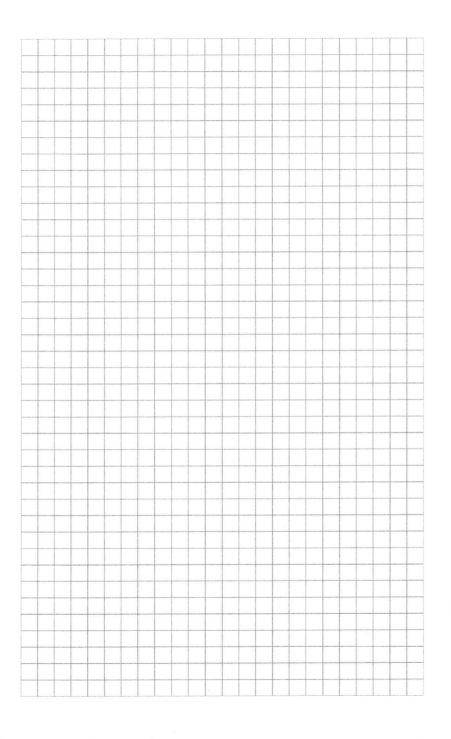

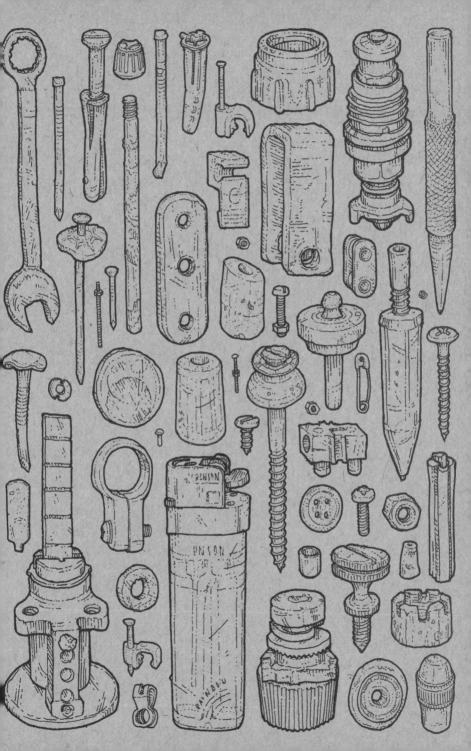

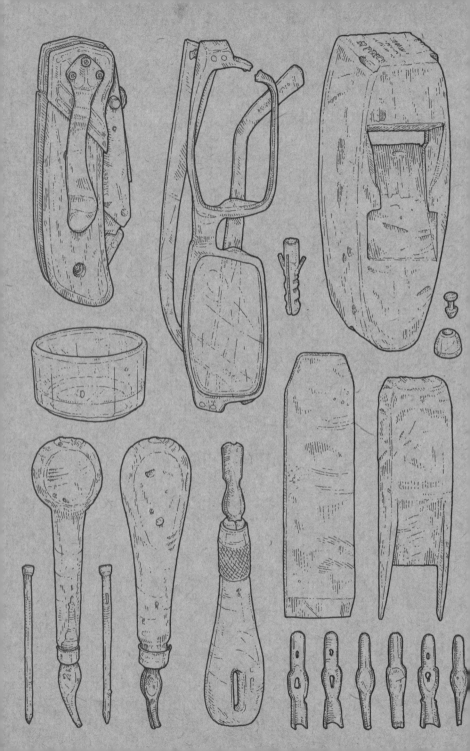

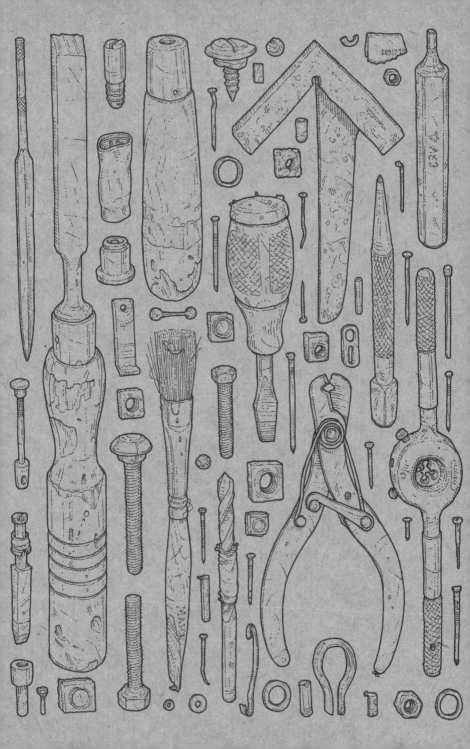

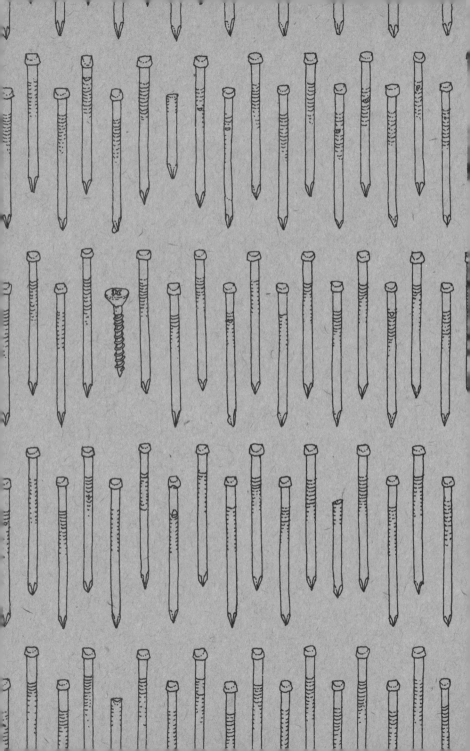

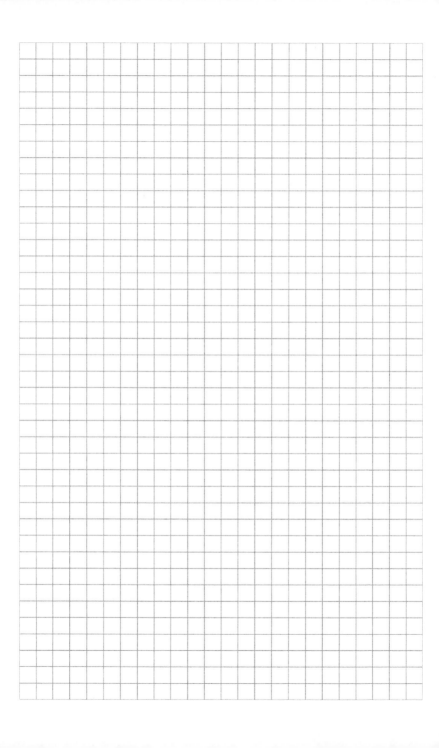

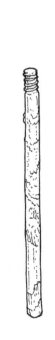

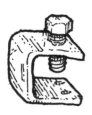

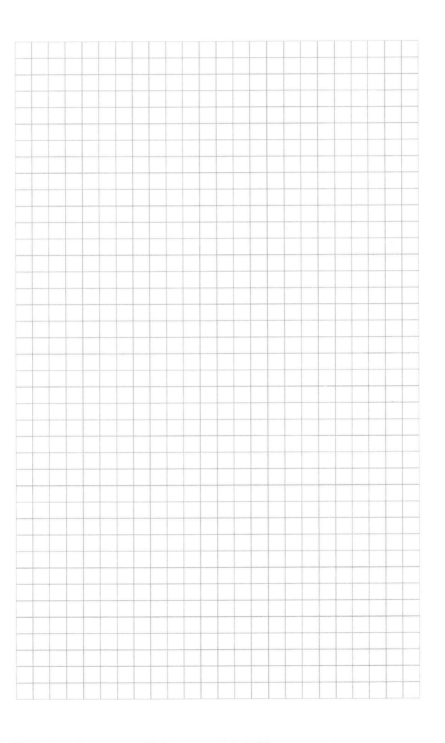

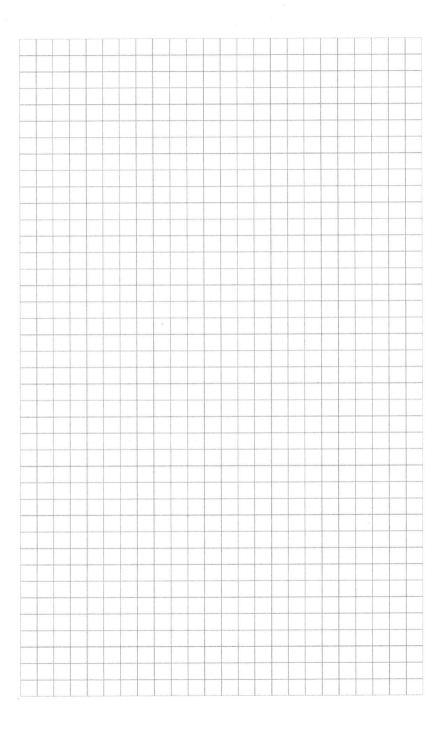

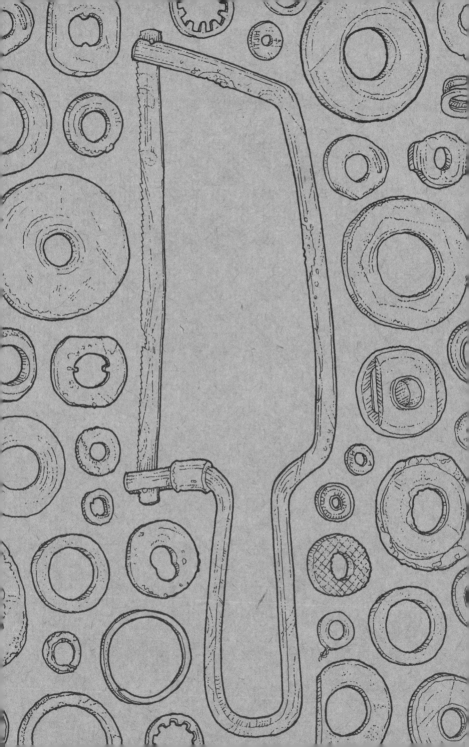

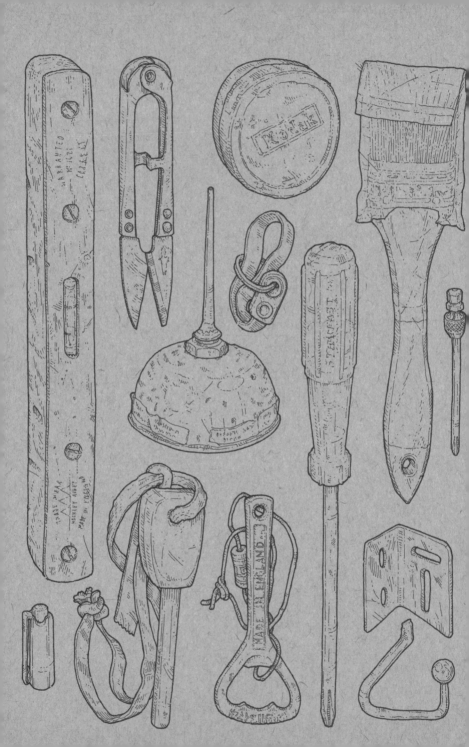

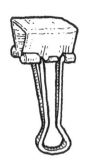

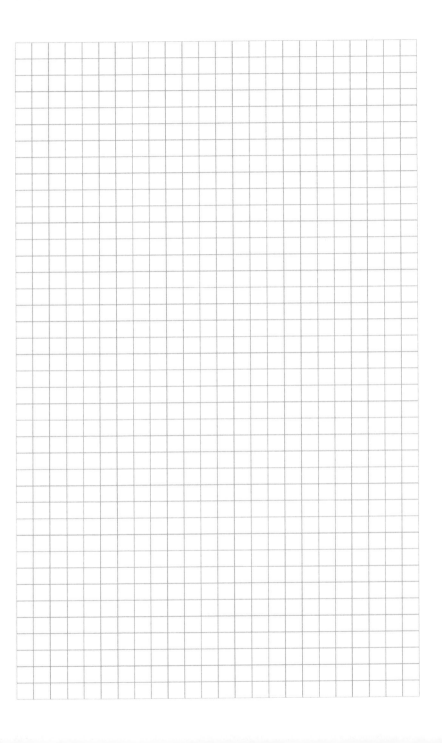

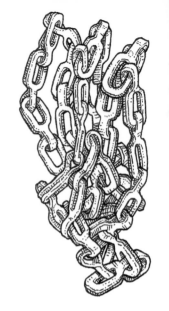

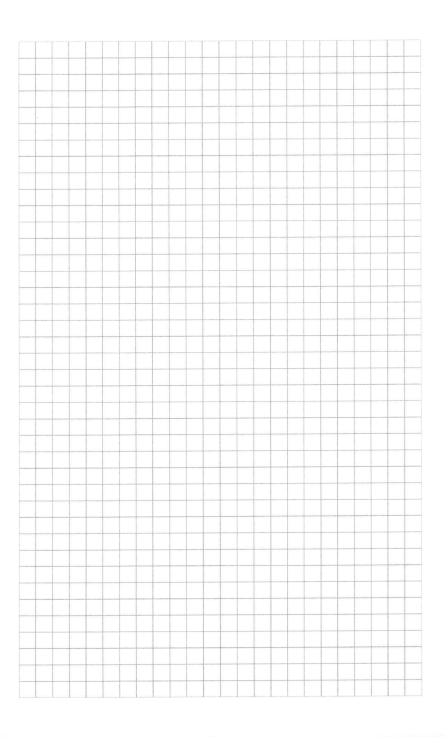

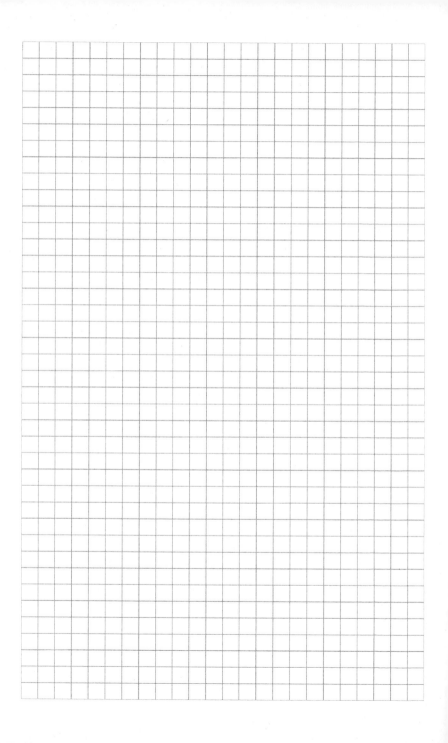

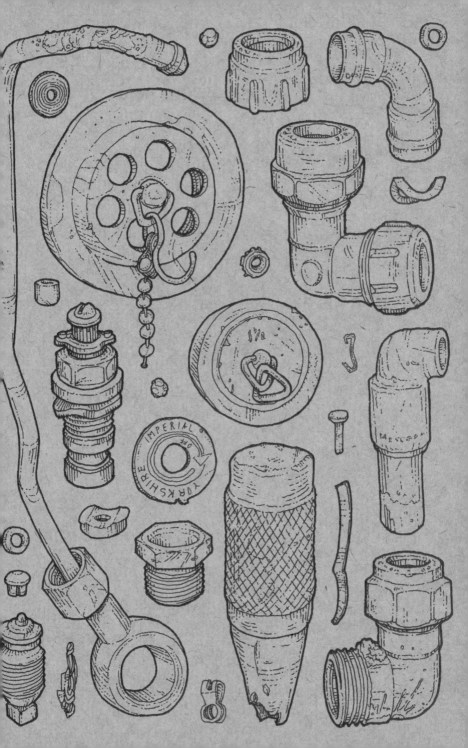

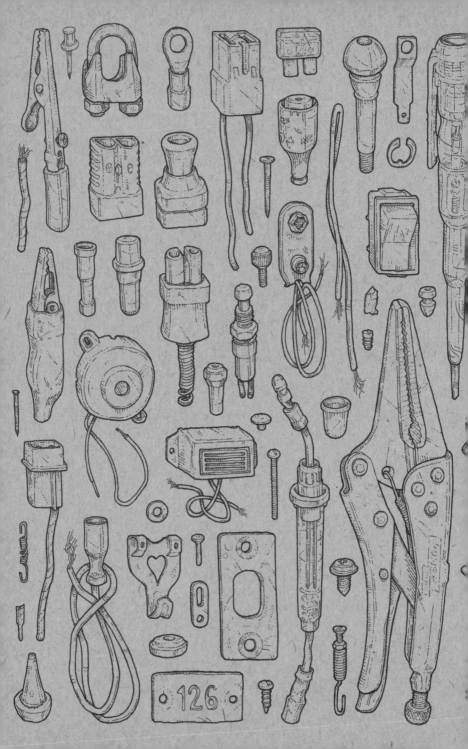

126

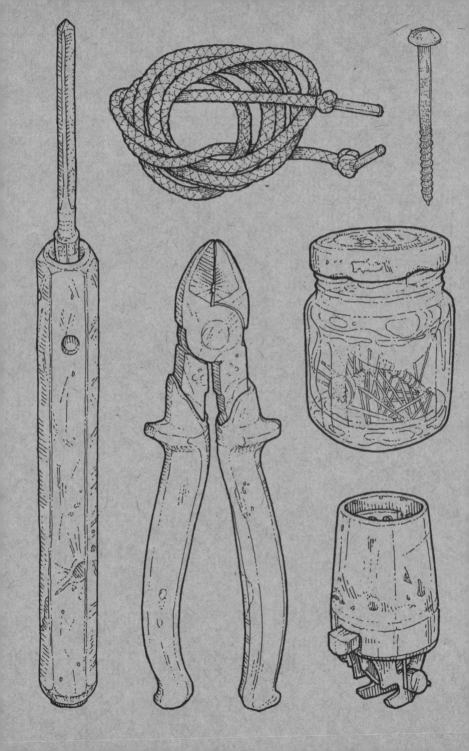

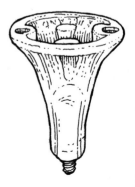

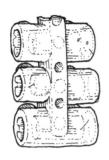

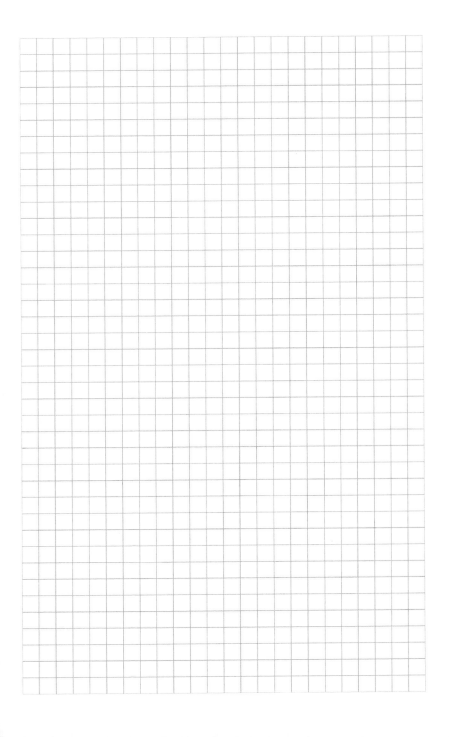

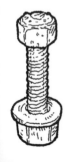

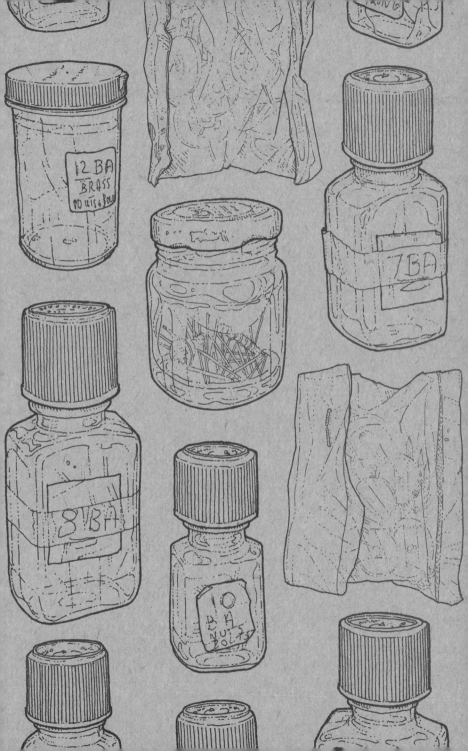

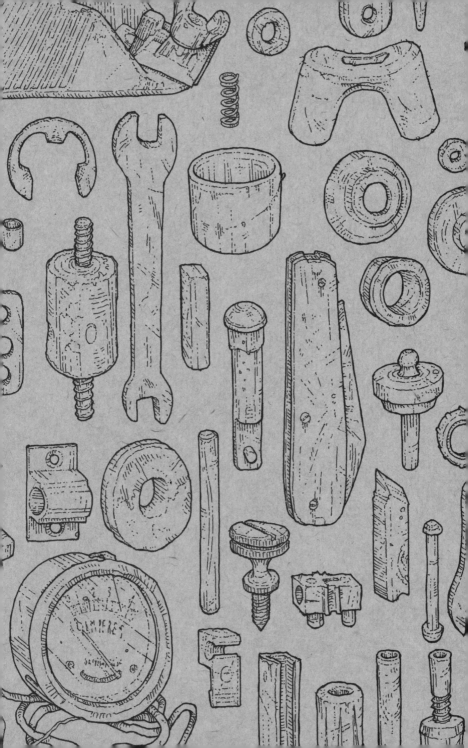

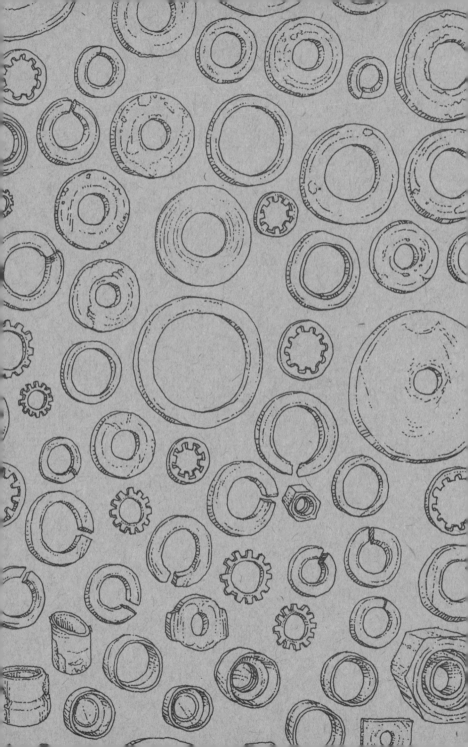

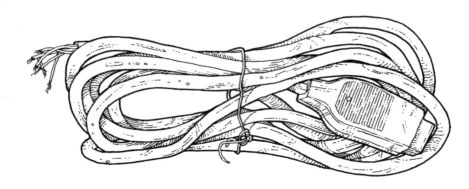

LEE JOHN PHILLIPS
THE SHED PROJECT

My grandfather, Handel Jones, died in
1994. His shed has remained relatively
untouched. My grandmother treats it
as a mausoleum.

He was a practical man and would spend
a great deal of time in that shed
fixing, salvaging and making. Broken
items were stripped of their parts
and components sorted into relevant
containers. Nothing was thrown away.

In 2013 I completed one drawing a day in
the same sketchbook for the whole year.
I decided that 2014 would see me
complete an item a day from the
shed in a similar fashion.

I made a decision that every item would
be given equal importance, regardless
of how small or seemingly insignificant.
I made myself some rules:

1. If the item can be picked up and
   doesn't crumble if rubbed, draw it.

2. If the packet/container is/has been
   opened, empty it, draw items,
   replace them, draw the container full.

3. If the packet/container has not
   been opened, it will not be, and
   drawn as found.

4. If there are multiples of the same
   items, draw them all.

I estimate there to be over 100,000
items. To date, I have drawn over 4,600.

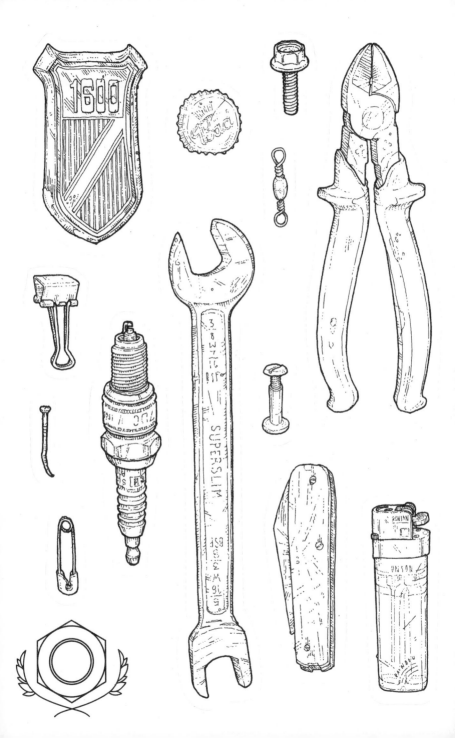